THE ANCIENT WORLD

The Vikings

THE ANCIENT WORLD

The Vikings

Pamela Odijk

Silver Burdett Press

Acknowledgments

The author and publishers are grateful to the following for permission to reproduce copyright photographs and prints:

ANT/NHPA pp. 13, 14; Coo-ee Picture Library p. 11; Ron Sheridan's Photo-Library pp. 9, 10, 15, 16, 17, 27 right, 26, 28; Stock Photos p. 41; Universitetets Oldsaksamling pp. 18, 32; Werner Forman Archive pp. 12, 20, 27 left, 24, 31, 33, 34, 36, 39, 40 and the cover photograph.

While every care has been taken to trace and acknowledge copyright, the publishers tender their apologies for any accidental infringement where copyright has proved untraceable. They would be pleased to come to a suitable arrangement with the rightful owner in each case.

© Pamela Odijk 1989

All rights reserved. No part of this publication
may be reproduced or transmitted, in any
form or by any means, without permission.

First published 1989 by
THE MACMILLAN COMPANY OF AUSTRALIA PTY LTD
107 Moray Street, South Melbourne 3205
6 Clarke Street, Crows Nest 2065

Adapted and first published in the United States in 1990
by Silver Burdett Press, Englewood Cliffs, N.J.

Library of Congress Cataloging-in-Publication Data

Odijk, Pamela, 1942–
    The Vikings / by Pamela Odijk
      p. cm. — (The Ancient World)
    Summary: Describes the culture, religion, literature, daily life,
and voyages of the Vikings and why the civilization declined after
300 years.
    1. Vikings — Juvenile literature. 2. Northmen — Juvenile
literature. [1. Vikings.] I. Title. II. Series: Odijk, Pamela, 1942–
Ancient World.
DL65.035 1990
948'.022 — dc20   89-38601
ISBN 0-382-09893-5   CIP
                                                                              AC

The Vikings

Contents

The Vikings: Timeline 6
The Vikings: Introduction 9
The Importance of Landforms and Climate 11
Natural Plants, Animals, and Birds 13
Crops, Herds, and Hunting 14
How Families Lived 16
Food and Medicine 19
Clothes 20
Religion and Rituals of the Vikings 23
Obeying the Law 27
Writing It Down: Recording Things 28
Viking Legends and Literature 30
Art and Architecture 32
Going Places: Transportation, Exploration, and Communication 34
Music, Dancing, and Recreation 36
Wars and Battles 37
Viking Inventions and Special Skills 39
Why the Civilization Declined 41
Glossary 42
The Vikings: Some Famous People and Places 44
Index 46

The Vikings: Timeline

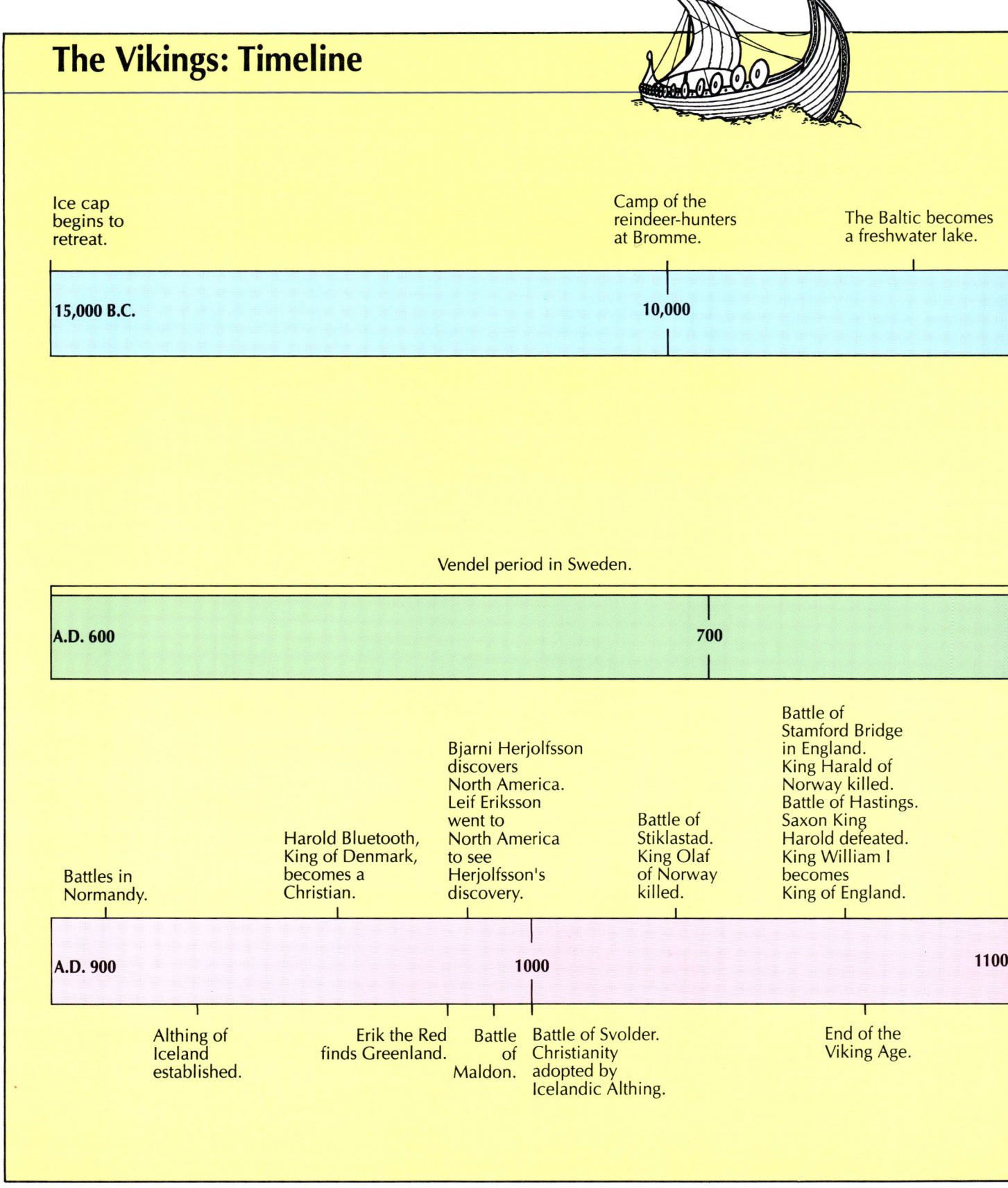

Ice cap begins to retreat.

Camp of the reindeer-hunters at Bromme.

The Baltic becomes a freshwater lake.

15,000 B.C. — 10,000

Vendel period in Sweden.

A.D. 600 — 700

Battles in Normandy.

Harold Bluetooth, King of Denmark, becomes a Christian.

Bjarni Herjolfsson discovers North America. Leif Eriksson went to North America to see Herjolfsson's discovery.

Battle of Stiklastad. King Olaf of Norway killed.

Battle of Stamford Bridge in England. King Harald of Norway killed. Battle of Hastings. Saxon King Harold defeated. King William I becomes King of England.

A.D. 900 — 1000 — 1100

Althing of Iceland established.

Erik the Red finds Greenland.

Battle of Maldon.

Battle of Svolder. Christianity adopted by Icelandic Althing.

End of the Viking Age.

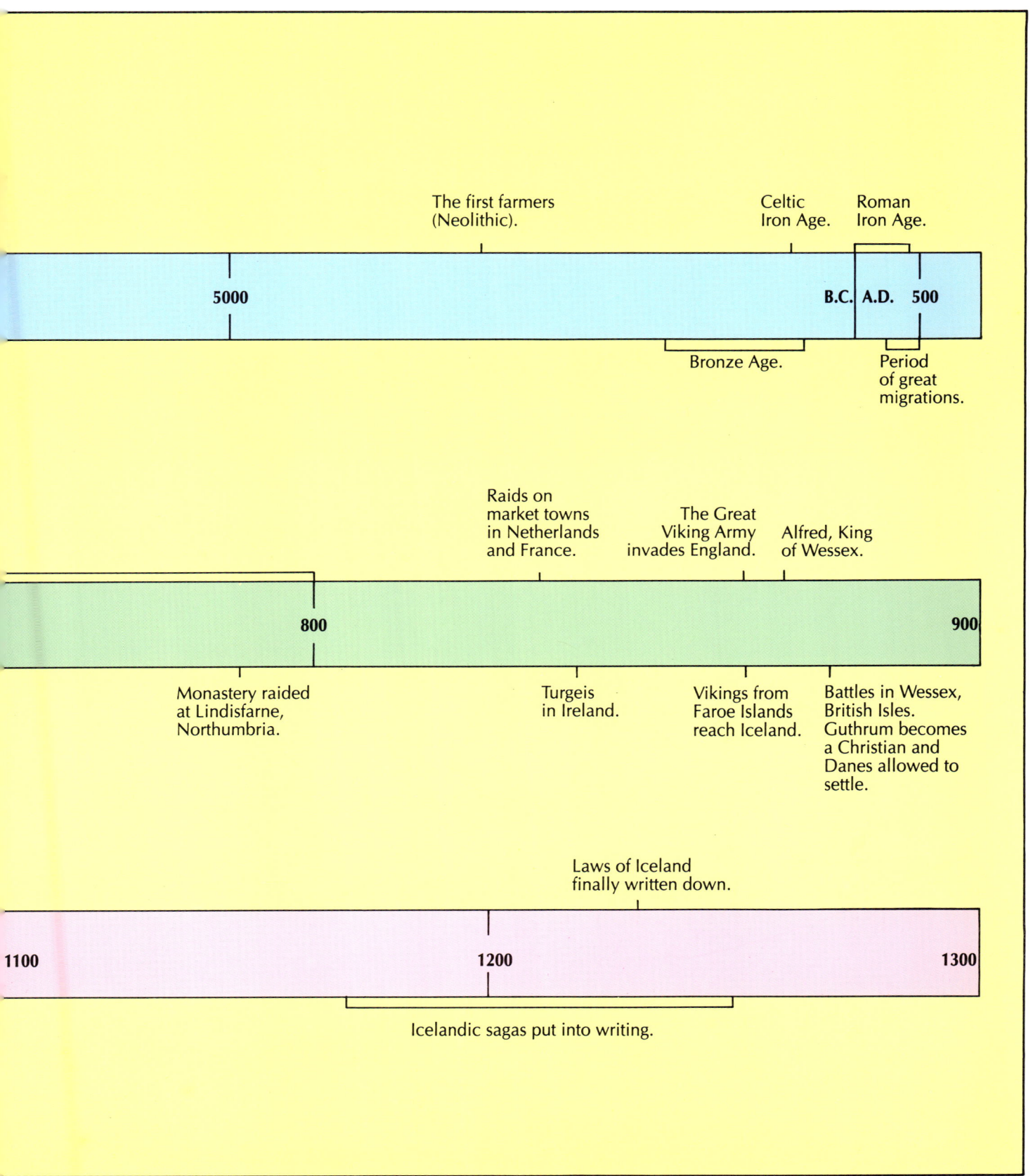

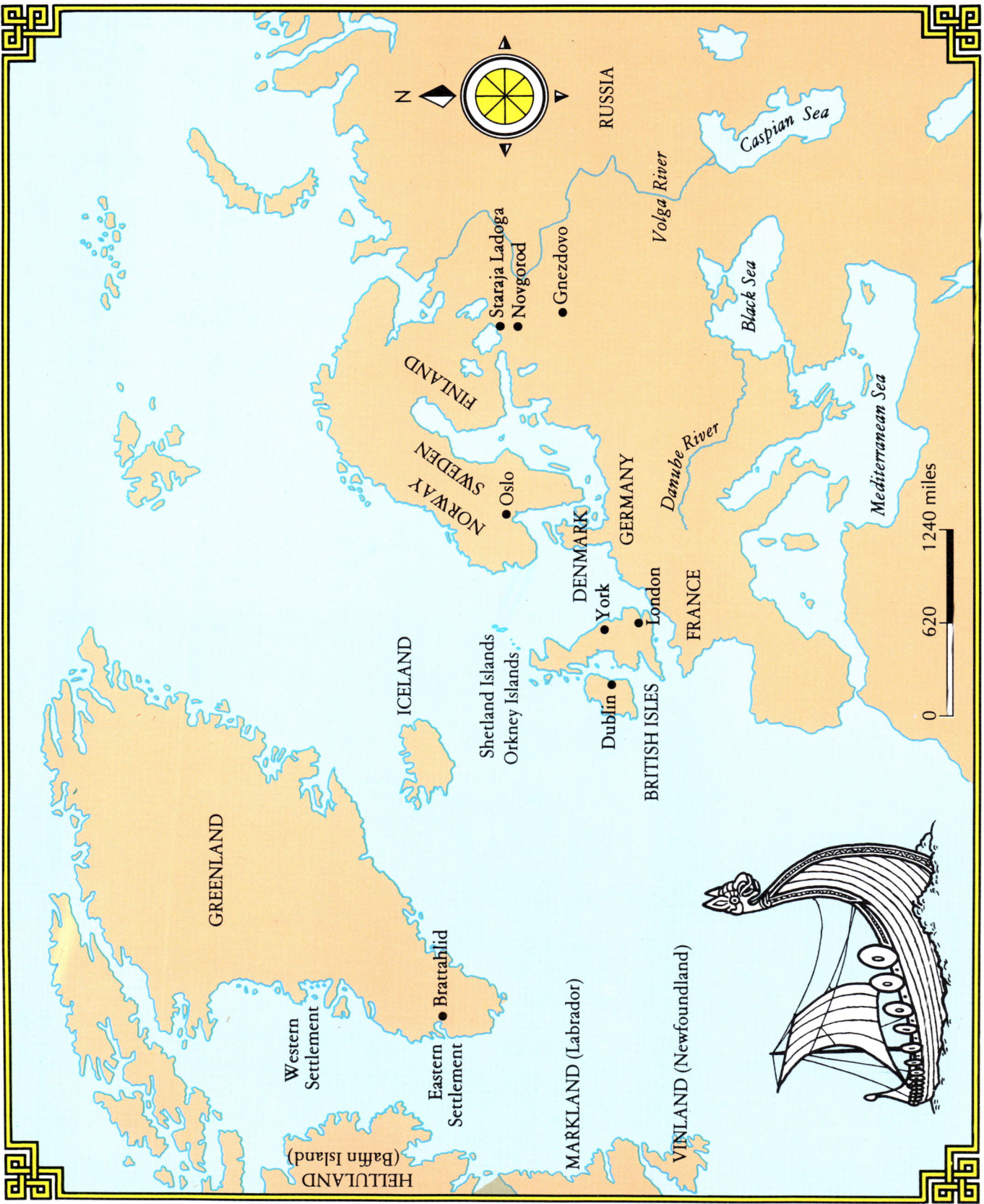

The Vikings: Introduction

The Vikings, also called the Norsemen and, in Russia, the Varangians, came from the cold Scandinavian lands of Denmark, Sweden, and Norway. The Germans called them arcomanni or "ship-men," the Arabs in Spain called them el-Majus or "the **heathen**." The Irish monks called the Norwegians the Finn-gaill or "white foreigners." The two main types of Scandinavians have always been easily recognized: the tall, fair-haired, blue-eyed people and the short, dark-skinned, brown or dark-haired, broad-faced people. Each took a different route upon leaving the homeland. Those from Norway went west to the northern British Isles, Iceland, and Greenland. Those from Denmark went southwest to England, France, and northern Germany, and those from Sweden went into Finland and Russia.

The Viking Age lasted from about A.D. 780 to 1070 and it was during this time that the Vikings moved overseas. They were warriors as well as traders. They traveled widely, both on raids, and in search of trade. The Vikings developed important trade routes, and were the first to journey across the Atlantic to America. They had great influence on the government and culture of the countries they invaded.

The harsh, cold climate of Scandinavia made the land hard to farm, so the Vikings also traveled in search of more land to farm and on which to graze stock. Like other people Vikings desired wealth and luxury goods that became available as trade routes opened. They built fine ships and market towns to make this possible. They also used invasion and conquest to obtain material goods, and to give power and importance to rulers and leaders.

Detail from a carved funerary stone showing ship full of Viking warriors, tenth century A.D.

The Vikings were great poets and storytellers. Our knowledge of their culture comes from three sources: **archaeology**, numismatics (the study of coins and medals), and written records.

The Viking contribution to European trade eventually made possible the northward expansion of Christian European civilization. Christian missionaries, sent to Scandinavian

countries, began to preach against the Viking way of life, particularly the Viking and Muslim slave trade. Eventually some leaders were converted to Christianity, their people ordered to follow their example, and thus the Viking way of life was dramatically changed.

Also, weak states, easily conquered by the earlier Vikings, built up defenses, and the Turks, too, began to move into eastern lands and trade routes. By the eleventh century A.D the Vikings ceased to control any part of England.

The Viking Age ended for several reasons. The three main Scandinavian countries, from which the Vikings came, were not really organized into one fighting force. In fact, the Norsemen often fought among themselves making defeat by other countries possible. Also, other countries had learned to build ships of equal if not better quality, and could defeat the Vikings at sea. The gradual conversion of the Vikings to Christianity meant that the Viking Age the world had known for 300 years was over.

Broch of Gurness in Orkney, Scotland: Viking ruins of a wall and interior with well, stairs, and partition.

The Importance of Landforms and Climate

The landforms and climate of any area determine to a large extent how people live, what kinds of crops can be grown and where, and what kinds of animals can be raised.

The Scandinavian lands are very mountainous, especially in Norway and Sweden, which means that very little land is available for cultivation and grazing. Only 3 percent of the land in Norway, 9 percent in Sweden, and 50 percent of the land in Denmark could be farmed, as much of the soil in these countries was very poor.

All of Scandinavia lies in the cold area of the world where in winter there are only a few hours of daylight, and in summer, although days are long, the season is short and still quite

The Scandinavian lands are very mountainous, leaving little land for growing crops and raising animals.

Sogne Fjord, western Norway—this fjord is 4,050 feet (1,234 meters) deep and is typical of the coastline of one of the lands once inhabited by the Vikings.

cool. For part of each year, large areas are covered with ice and snow. This means that the growing season is short and land on which to grow crops is limited. Having suitable land for grazing and sufficient shelter were always problems for farmers. People looked to other sources for food, such as fishing along the coastline. In places like Norway, the coastline is very rugged with many **fjords**.

The lack of good farmland for the increasing population is thought to be one reason why the Vikings set out to seek new lands. The land in warmer climates of Europe and Britain was ideal for farming. Also these lands had commodities which the Scandinavians could not produce in their own countries.

Natural Plants, Animals, and Birds

Plants that grew naturally and animals and birds that lived among them were also important. With limited farmland the Scandinavians learned to make use of the animals available.

Most land in the cold mountains and **glacial valleys** was covered with dense pine and other forests. Because wood was plentiful it was used for building houses and boats, and for making firewood, **charcoal**, furniture, and utensils.

By studying animals in the wild, Norsemen learned to trap them for food and fur. Animals such as reindeer, wolverines, lemmings, elk, red deer, bears, lynx, and seals were found.

Birds, including partridges and grouse, found their way to Viking lands on their migration routes and were caught. Eggs of seabirds were also collected.

Trout, salmon, cod, and herring were among the fish that were regularly caught.

Wolverines inhabit the dense pine forests where the Vikings lived.

13

Crops, Herds, and Hunting

The Vikings returned to their families and farms at the end of each sea voyage. While Vikings were at sea, their families ran the farms. Family life was organized according to the seasons.

In the short growing season, fields were plowed with horse- or ox-drawn plows and planted with rye, oats, wheat, corn, and barley. Like peasants elsewhere, families performed rituals to ensure a good harvest. The Scandinavian custom was for the farmer's wife to bake a cake made in the shape of the sun. This cake was carried with a tankard of ale or mead (a drink made from fermented honey and water) to the stables where draft animals were kept. All animals and workmen ate a piece of cake, and the rest was crumbled and put in the seed box to be planted with the seed. Each workman drank from the tankard and the rest of the ale was poured over the animals. In some places in Sweden this custom is still practiced.

Vegetables, such as cabbages, peas, and beans, were grown in smaller garden plots. The **flax** plant also was cultivated.

The Vikings hunted the bull reindeer using spears and bows and arrows.

Items not produced on farms were obtained by trade. Such items included pottery vessels, hard millstones, glassware dishes, and goblets.

When Vikings **colonized** lands in the Hebrides, Shetland, and Orkney Islands, they set up farms in much the same way as they had done in their homelands.

Herds

Cattle, sheep, pigs, and poultry were kept for food, wool, hides, and feathers. Herd animals were taken to the mountain pastures to graze during the warm summer months; families often had small summer farmhouses. Shepherds and sheepdogs watched the sheep. At the beginning of the cold autumn months, the animals would be taken from the mountains (which would soon be covered with snow) and housed in animal shelters on the farms. Domesticated cats and dogs were also kept. Dogs were particularly useful for watching sheep, guarding the home, and hunting game.

When a farmer was called to sea or to fight, a ceremony was held to transfer the house keys from the husband to his wife. This ceremony symbolized the wife's authority over the house, land, and animals and all farm workers. Many farms resembled huge estates, and the planning and directing of them was a complicated task. Responsibility for house and dairy routines also had to be assumed.

Hunting and Fishing

Deer, elk, wild boars, bears, rabbits, and game birds were hunted, along with whales, reindeer, polar bears, and seals in the more northerly regions. These animals were hunted with spears and bows and arrows.(The Scandinavian bow, which is very effective, was later used in Ireland.) Animals were used for other things besides food. Antlers, bones, and hides were used for clothing and tents. Hunting was frequently done on horseback. The Vikings were particularly fond of horses. They cared for them well and often made quite decorative saddles, bridles, and spurs. Hunting with falcons was a Viking pastime.

Along the coast, fish were caught with lines and traps, and shellfish were collected. Boats were used for deep-sea fishing.

Iron stirrup with brass inlay dated from late tenth to eleventh century. The Vikings also made decorative saddles, bridles, and spurs.

How Families Lived

Families were important to the Vikings and often the inhabitants of an entire village would belong to only a few families. Family loyalty was strong. Ancestors were considered part of the living family. Households also had a number of slaves called **thralls**.

Houses

Houses and other buildings were made of wood and had thatched roofs. Some houses eleven yards (ten meters) in length, with a high pitched roof, were known as long-houses. One main building, called a **stofa**, was used for eating and sleeping. It had a huge fireplace in the center. Tables and benches were carried in for meals. Benches along the walls were used as beds at night. The main building was decorated with shields and tapestries. Other farm buildings, called **burs**, which sometimes had sleeping lofts, were used for sheltering animals, and storing grain, hay, equipment, and tools. Also room for a blacksmith and a dairy was available.

In some houses sleeping areas were separated from the rest of the house by a thick curtain. Square wooden beds had mattresses of straw and were covered with blankets and quilts filled with duck and goose feathers. The Vikings did not have glass windows and probably used animal membranes stretched over a frame.

Furniture was often beautifully carved and had many cushions and pillows for comfort.

Reconstruction of a Viking village at York, England.

Men

Most Norsemen were farmers. It was only when the farm work of plowing and sowing was finished that the young men went off in the boats "a-viking," which was the way the Scandinavians described this seafaring way of life. Young men from fourteen or fifteen years of age onwards could go to sea. The head of the farm or village had to ensure that the community and farms operated properly, and that enough food was produced and stored for the winter months. Wood for cooking and for winter fires had to be cut and stored.

Women

Viking women also were involved in the farming. Women milked the cows and goats and made butter and cheese, which was stored in underground cellars. In the autumn many cattle, sheep, and goats were slaughtered and the women would salt and store the meat. Fish were also preserved. Foods were pickled in brine and vinegar.

Women also did the spinning, weaving, and dyeing of wool and flax. They sewed, embroidered, and made clothes. Other household tasks, including the cleaning, preparing, and cooking of daily meals, were done by women. Besides looking after the farm when husbands were at sea, Viking women would also defend the home against attack and trade with visiting merchants.

Children

From an early age, children had to assist with community and family activities. There were no Viking schools. Children were taught skills by other adults. At about seven to eight years of age boys were often sent to the house of foster parents. The ties between natural and foster parents bound families together that were not related by blood and made sure that boys were given a disciplined upbringing.

Ruins of Viking buildings in Brough of Birsay, Orkney, Scotland.

The Gokstad ship—since Vikings traveled long distances by sea, much time was spent living on boats.

Thralls

The Vikings were slave traders, as were many people in bygone eras. Thralls were the slaves of the household or community. People became thralls either by being captured on raids, as a punishment for certain crimes, or by being born into thralldom.

The thralls were given work to do in the house or the fields. Viking law stated that any farm large enough to have twelve cows and two horses should have at least three thralls.

Thralls seem to have been reasonably well treated and some families were known to have given thralls their freedom as a gift.

Life on Board a Viking Ship

Each sailor was given a sea chest in which to secure his belongings. The chest also served as a rowing seat. Sleeping bags made out of leather were used on board or laid out on beaches. A large tent, which could cover the whole ship or could be taken ashore and set up like an awning, was taken on board also. Portable board games also were carried by the Vikings.

Food and Medicine

Food

Food was cooked in a kitchen or fire house, called a **skali** or **eld-hus**, which was separate from the living quarters. Most cooking in the skali was done over an open hearth (fire).

Grain was ground into flour for making whole grain breads. Porridge was made from oatmeal, barley, and eggs, with honey being used as a sweetener. Soups and stews were cooked in iron cauldrons over the fire, and quarters of meat were roasted on spits or fried in iron pans. Food was seasoned with salt from the sea, and pepper and spices brought back by traders.

Dairy foods, butter, cheese, and a creamy curd called **skyr** were eaten. Fish, either salted, fresh, or smoked, was a common food.

Milk and buttermilk were favorite drinks. Ale, mead, and wine were brewed.

Food at Sea

The Vikings at sea had to find ways of making food nutritious. It seems they managed to do this well, for illnesses such as **scurvy** and **beriberi**, diseases common to sailors elsewhere, were unknown among the Vikings.

Cooking could not be done on board Viking ships, so food was precooked and eaten cold. Each boat carried a huge iron cauldron, which was used to cook food on the beaches. Water, beer, and mead were carried in skin bags.

Medicine

We do not have much information about Viking medical cures; but, the people seem to have been free of many diseases that occurred

Cooking in the eld-hus was done over an open hearth.

elsewhere. Since Vikings were particular about cleanliness, ate a well-balanced diet, and led very active lives, they remained in very good health. The cold climate of Scandinavia also helped prevent the spread of many diseases.

Clothes

The Scandinavians were practical people who liked bright colors and ornaments. This is shown by the clothes they wore which were of three types: work and everyday clothes, special occasion clothes, and for the men, battle dress and seagoing clothes. Materials used in making clothing included home-woven wool, fine wool brought back from the Netherlands, linen, and fur. Silk was obtained by trade with Russia. A large piece of silk damask interwoven with gold thread was found aboard the Gokstad ship. Woven wool, and looms for making braids and laces, were found aboard the Oseberg ship. These ships are now on display in the Viking Ship Museum in Oslo.

Men's Clothing

Men wore long linen underwear with thick trousers on top. Long underwear was used also as pajamas. A long-sleeved shirt made from wool or linen was worn, and over it went a knee-length tunic called a **kyrtil**. Kyrtils worn for special occasions were brightly colored, often scarlet, and trimmed with fur. Men sometimes wore kilts similar to those worn by the Scots. Beards, moustaches, and shoulder-length hair were worn as protection from the cold. Both men and women wore hats. Men's hats were either round, wool, stiffened hats, called **skalhatts**, or wide-brimmed hats for wearing in the fields. Wealthier people could afford Russian hats and a fur-lined cloak called a **möttul**, that was fastened with a brooch.

Women's Clothing

Women wore a linen or silk vest under a long-sleeved tunic. A rectangular pinafore reaching to the knee was worn over the tunic. Clothing was held in place by straps and brooches. Chains, held in place with brooches, were often draped for hanging useful things such as keys, scissors, and a money purse. For everyday use a linen apron was worn. Women were also fond of bright colors.

A woman's hair style defined her status. An unmarried or widowed woman had long, uncovered hair, and a married woman tucked her hair beneath a white linen, embroidered scarf.

Young girls often wore short skirts.

Both men and women wore heavy cloaks with fur-lined hoods called **kapas**. Shoes were leather kneeboots or dress shoes of soft hide lined with silk and decorated with gold.

Jewelry

Jewelry was worn as a sign of wealth and for decoration. Silver and gold jewelry was common. Brooches, such as the one shown opposite, were used to hold items of clothing in place.

Opposite: silver-plated iron brooch with enamel work and precious stones.

Clothes at Sea

The practical Vikings adapted their clothing to suit their seafaring life. On the cold seas they wore heavy woolen or leather trousers, a sleeveless leather jerkin, or a hip-length fur-lined coat. The clothes worn on top were made of oiled skin, which made them waterproof. Their long, hooded cloaks and capes also could be used as blankets.

Sailors often fastened cloth sacks to their trouser legs. They also wore leather boots with fur linings for winter. Gloves and woolen caps protected hands and heads from the cold.

Battle Dress

The Vikings' battle dress was designed for ease of movement. Battle helmets were made from leather and sometimes covered in iron. Other decorative helmets, such as those with horns or shaped like birds, were for ceremonies. These ceremonial hats would have been uncomfortable in battle, and in some cases, dangerous.

Above: gold jewelry worn by the Vikings, including brooches, armlets, necklaces, and bracelets.

Below: tenth century leather boot from York, England. Usually leather boots were lined with fur for the cold winter weather.

Religion and Rituals of the Vikings

Important Asar Gods

Odin (sometimes called Woden) chief of gods, god of battle who ruled Asgard, home of the gods. He is depicted as a mysterious one-eyed god.

Thor. Odin's son, god of thunder, war, and strength. He carried a huge stone hammer called mjollnir.

Tyr Odin's son, god of war.

Balder Odin's son, god of youth, beauty and goodness.

Loki a troublemaker. (Balder and Loki were not friends.)

Important Vanir Gods

Mimir guard of the well of wisdom at the root of the tree Yggdrasil.

Njord ruler of wind and god of seafaring.

Frey Njord's son, god of fertility who gave good crops and ensured the survival of the race. At the great midwinter feast, a boar was always sacrificed to Frey and its head carried in procession.

Freyja Njord's daughter, goddess of love and beauty, who was always attended by cats.

The Vikings worshiped many gods. Gods were believed to assist with the growth of crops and to help them in battle. These gods were from two families, called Asar (Aesir) and Vanir, which appear above.

Supposedly, Odin gave up one of his eyes in exchange for a drink from Mimir's Well of Knowledge, beneath Yggdrasil's Ash Tree. Odin also had two ravens named Hugin and Mugin (Thought and Memory). Each day the ravens would fly around the world and return at night to tell Odin all they had seen. Odin, at times, disguised himself as an old man in a wide-brimmed hat and cloak. Adopting the name Grim, he pleaded with Christians to return to their old ways of worship.

Some places in England and elsewhere still bear the names of gods from whom they were derived. Our days of the week are also named after them: *Tyr's day, Woden's day, Thor's day,* and *Frey's day,* to name a few.

Yggdrasil Ash Tree

According to the Vikings, this tree held up the sky and the gods lived beneath it in their home of Asgarth. The long roots of the tree extended into Midgarth (the world of mankind), the world of the Frost Giants, and the world of the dead, called Hel.

At the tree's root was the Well of Knowledge and the Well of Fate. At the Well of Fate lived three Norns—Past, Present, and Future—who wove a huge cloth in which every thread represented a person's life. When someone died his thread in the cloth was cut.

Festivals

The Vikings made animal sacrifices to the gods, especially during the three main festivals:

Vetrarblot—mid-October, when sacrifices were made to ensure a good winter.
Jolablot or **Midsvetrarblot**—mid-January when sacrifices were made to ensure good crops. Boars, Frey's sacred animals, were always sacrificed to him.
Sigrblot—in April when sacrifices were made for victories at war.

At these festivals people ate horsemeat and drank bowls of wine. Sometimes animals were not killed but rather were dedicated to the god. The owner could then continue using the animal.

After Death

The Vikings believed that after death the spirits of the good were rewarded and the spirits of the bad were punished. The spirit was supposed to sail to a new life. Many important people were buried at sea or in ships with their possessions. Those who were buried on land sometimes had stones placed around their graves in the shape of a ship. In Iceland, graves with boats or ships are rare. Here the main way to travel was by horse, and over two-thirds of Icelandic graves have the remains of one or more horses buried with the person.

Opposite: woven tapestry which shows the Norse gods, Odin, Thor, and Frey. Odin carries his axe, Thor his hammer, and Frey an ear of corn. Odin's name was bestowed on very few places but he is well remembered in literature and was regarded as the god of poetry. He was also the god of wisdom. Thor was a god common to all early Germanic peoples and was sometimes regarded as secondary to Odin and, in some traditions, as Odin's son. Place names in England suggest that Thor (or Thunor, as he was called in English) was well known in Saxon and Jutish areas. Frey had other names as well, Yngi or Yngvi-Freyr and was the imaginary father of north Germanic tribes. He was worshiped in Sweden especially and was well known in Norway and Iceland.

Brave warriors were supposed to go to Valhalla (Odin's paradise), to celebrate and await Ragnarök (the last battle that would bring about the end of the world).

Ragnarök—the End of the World

This would be the time when the gods would be killed by giants and monsters. The sign that this was about to happen would be three years of winter and three years of war. Huge wolves would then swallow the sun and the moon and the enormous serpent called Midgarthsorm, who was coiled around the earth, would rise up from the sea.

The watchman, Bifrost, who sat on the rainbow bridge leading to the land of Asgarth, would watch for the giants to come. When they appeared, his job was to summon the warriors from Valhalla even though it was known that they, too, would be overpowered. The wolf, Fenrir, would eat Odin; Thor would be poisoned by the serpent, which would also die; the Fire Giant, Surt, would kill Frey. The stars would then fall from the sky and the earth would sink into the sea. But, it was believed, some would survive, and those survivors would build a new and better world that would rise up out of the sea.

Temples

The Vikings built temples to their gods and descriptions of them can be found in the sagas and writings of the early Christians. One famous central temple was built and maintained by the Swedish kings at Uppsala, where a great religious celebration was held every ninth year. The temple stood beside three great burial mounds of the kings. After it was destroyed, the Christians built a church over it. Even today, people can go through the trap door of this church into the foundations of the old pagan Viking temple. This temple was still being used in A.D. 1070 and was the chief center of resistance to the new religion of Christianity.

Ruins of a Viking boat burial—sometimes stones were placed around the grave in the shape of a boat. Important people were buried either in these boat-shaped graves or in their boats at sea.

The Coming of Christianity

Missionaries were often sent from England and Germany to convert the Vikings to Christianity, but were often thrown out of the Viking lands. Often they left of their own accord as they were not able to convert the Vikings.

Eventually, some of the Viking kings saw that being a Christian would give them advantages when dealing with other Christian rulers in Europe. In about A.D. 960 Harald Bluetooth, King of Denmark, became a Christian and decreed that all his subjects were to become Christians also.

The Norwegians rejected Christianity and also rejected their king, Haakon the Good, as long as he tried to convert the people. But their new king, Olaf Tryggvason, also became a Christian and threatened to put to death anyone who refused to be converted. He held visiting Icelanders hostage until the people in Iceland accepted the new religion. The Icelanders eventually accepted Christianity but also continued to practice their old religion in secret. This practice was the decision of the **Althing**, their parliament and place of law.

The people of Sweden resisted the Christians until A.D. 1008, when their king became a Christian. Their traditional temple still remained until the twelfth century.

Obeying the Law

"With law shall the land be built and with lawlessness wasted away." This is what the Vikings said and believed.

Viking law applied to all free people (**karls**). Thralls or slaves had few rights under the law, but it seems that they were not treated badly by the families who owned them. Free people, including the chief person of a region (**jarls**), formed parliaments called **Things**, where all law was preserved, decided, judged, and spoken. The parliaments grew up around the communities they served. The head of every family had to go to the parliament, and wives went in place of husbands if they were away. People also came to listen. Before the coming of Christianity, the parliaments chose the king.

Viking law was not written down but memorized and spoken aloud. Frequently a community would choose a young man to study the law for two or three years. Upon completion he would then be their legal adviser.

The Vikings had many laws. There were laws regarding property boundaries, hunting rights, felling of trees, songwriting (making of love songs), turning people's butter sour, offenses against the person and the community, marriage, divorce, inheritance, religious observance, and fair fighting. The law was concerned with the dignity and value of the individual in the society and punishment was ordered accordingly.

Punishments and Settlements

In many cases the law was quite clear and punishment was based on a predetermined code. In other cases an offense was settled by a duel, with set rules for declaring winners and losers. Another way of settling a dispute was to put an individual through a painful ordeal, such as having to grasp hot metal. The person would be judged guilty or innocent depending on how the wound healed.

On the whole the Vikings were obedient to the laws, accepting the judgment of the parliament. They found it to be helpful in creating a stable, honest, and reasonably safe community.

The oldest parliament in the world, the Althing of Iceland, was established in A.D. 930. It met each year and thousands of people went to listen to the lawspeakers. At the annual meeting of the Althing, people were given an opportunity to exchange information about trade and events, as well as to engage in entertainment and storytelling. By the decision of the Althing in A.D. 1000, Christianity was adopted in Iceland as the official religion, although people were still allowed to practice their old religion. The laws of Iceland were finally written down in about A.D. 1230, after the Viking Age was over.

Danelaw

Danelaw referred to that part of England in which Danish, not English, law was followed. It included the lands conquered by Danes in Northumbria, East Anglia, the Five Boroughs of Stamford, Leicester, Derby, Nottingham, Lincoln, and the southwest midlands. The southern boundary was established by the treaty made in A.D. 886 between King Alfred and Guthram of East Anglia.

Writing It Down: Recording Things

Until Christianity became well-established, most Scandinavian traditions, legends, and laws were passed down orally from one generation to another. Their **sagas** and long poems were not written down until the Middle Ages, after Christian monks had taught some people to write in Latin on parchment.

The Vikings did have an alphabet, called a **runic alphabet**, which started just before or at the beginning of the Christian era. At first it had twenty-four letters (or phonetic symbols), but this was later changed to sixteen letters by A.D. 700. The alphabet was named the **futhark**,

Runes carved into stone, found on the Orkney Islands in Scotland.

for its first letters. Only some Vikings could read and write in **runes**.

It is not known exactly where or how this runic alphabet began but traces of Latin, Greek, Etruscan, and other languages can be found in it. Viking legend says that the alphabet was a gift from the god Odin. Because the writing was mainly vertical and diagonal strokes with no curves, it is thought to have been originally used for wood and stone carving. Runes were also considered to be magical. Supposedly, runes carved in small sticks were used for blessings, spells, and curses. Runic inscriptions have been found in several places ranging from Greenland to the Black Sea, and from the Isle of Man to Athens, although few have been found in Iceland. About 500 have been found in Denmark, about 750 in Norway, and about 3,000 in Sweden.

Vikings carved their runes in long ribbons that covered the surface of a stone. The runes were painted in bright colors and set beside public roadways for all to read.

Rune stones, showing the runic alphabet used by the Vikings.

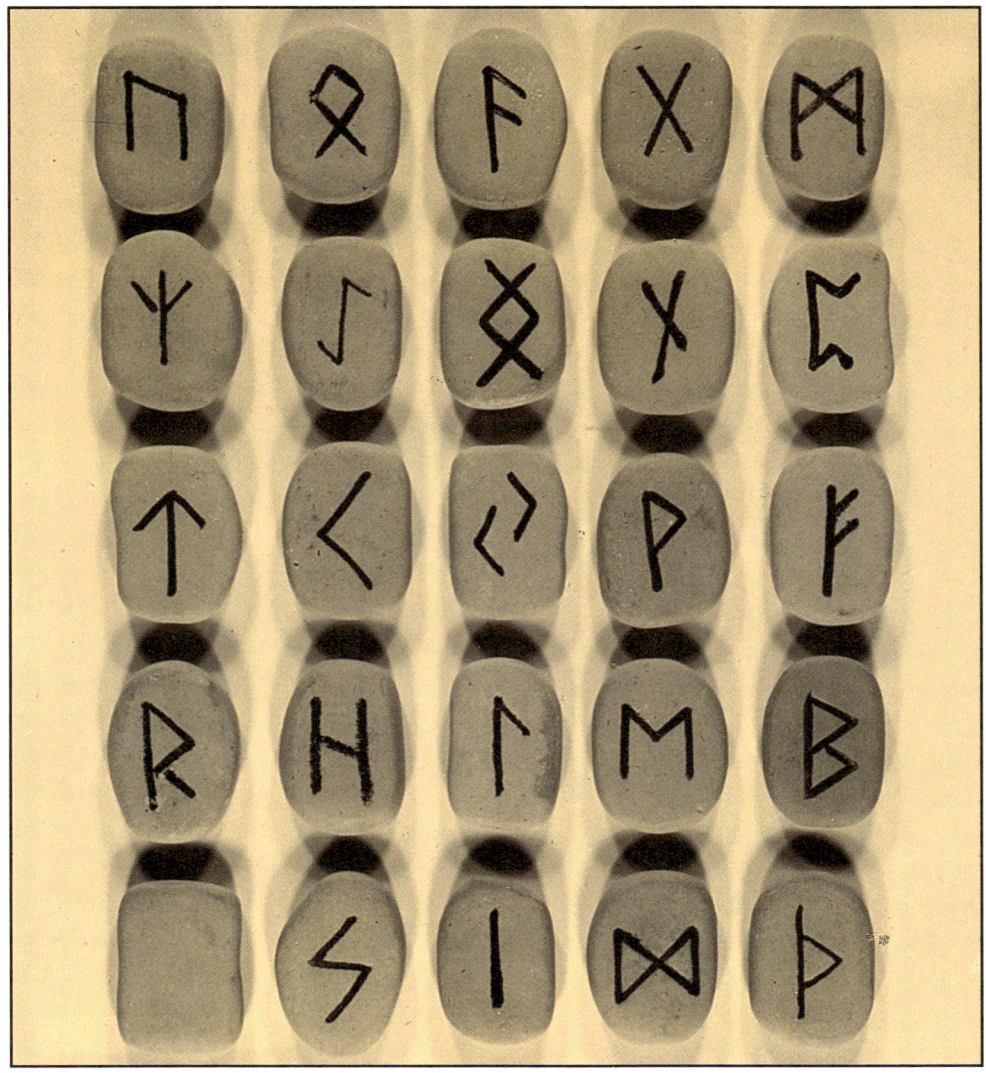

Viking Legends and Literature

Viking sagas were a mixture of fact and myth, designed mainly to entertain. Two of the best known, the Saga of Burnt Njal and the Laxdale Saga, have been translated into English. The most important sagas are referred to as the Sagas of the Norse Kings. They were collected Saemundr Sigfússon, who learned Latin as a priest in France, wrote a Latin history of the kings of Norway, but this history has since been lost. However, Ari Thorgilsson's *Islendingabók (Book of the Icelanders)* has survived, which covers about A.D. 118 to 870.

Some Legendary Sagas Name	What it is about
Njal's saga	Greatest of the sagas. About the characters of many people who come into contact with a farmer and his sage as they try to combat evil forces in society.
Edda	About the old gods of the north, including a tragic tale of Balder and a comic tale of Thor's journey into Giantland.
Grettis saga	About a hero who fights against heavy odds but who is finally slain.
Hœnsa-thoris saga	About a poor man who becomes rich as a peddler and decides to become a landowner but is unpopular.
Bandamanna saga	About chiefs who come to no good by trying to profit from other people's mistakes.
Eyrbyggja saga	About a feuding family.

and written down by an Icelander called Snorri Sturluson. The sagas, legends, and stories were passed on by word of mouth from one generation to another. They were not written down until long after the Viking Age ended.

The Vikings took great pleasure in listening to the **skalds** (poets and storytellers).

Histories

Scandinavian historians began to write about the Vikings after the Viking Age proper was over, near the end of the eleventh century A.D. Kolskeggr Asbjarnarson's *Landnámabók (Book of Settlement)* is another book that has survived. Others were also written.

Drapas

Poets who lived in the king's court wrote special poems, called **drapas**, in praise of the king. These poets were well rewarded for their efforts.

Above: detail of carved portal of Hyllestad Stavechurch, Setesdal—scene from the story of Sigurd, where he kills the dragon. Such legends represented Viking ideals of courage, bravery, ruthlessness, and cunning.

Right: Thor hammer pendant.

Art and Architecture

The Vikings acquired many beautiful objects by way of trade, but they also produced art of their own. They made intricate ornaments by melting down gold and silver, which were obtained through trade. The Vikings were excellent metal craftsmen and produced ornaments and beautifully crafted and decorated weapons. Animals were a favorite subject of Scandinavian artists.

Carved headpost from the Oseberg ship.

Woodcarving

The Vikings were excellent woodcarvers. Wood was plentiful and many everyday things were made from it, including dishes, troughs, casks, buckets, and furniture. Most furniture had intricately carved designs. The contents of the Gokstad and Oseberg ships are examples of the Viking woodcarver's art. The Oseberg ship's prow, the wagons, three sledges, and other items on board were made by artists of the early ninth century A.D. Some of the carvings on these items tell a story.

Picture Stones

In Gotland, Sweden, there are hundreds of memorial stones, which were produced from the fifth century A.D. on. These show many things, such as ships going on voyages, men fighting in battle, and warriors being welcomed to Valhalla. These stones depict the history of an era and thus are the art galleries of the Viking Age.

Architecture

No examples of kings' halls, temples, hill forts, or farm buildings have survived, as these were built of wood and easily destroyed. But archaeological evidence shows that the Vikings erected their buildings with good proportions, solid workmanship, and high artistic finish, which would have matched that of their Viking ships.

Shipbuilding

Perhaps the works which best show both the Viking artistry and superb engineering design are the Viking ships themselves. In recent years several of these ships have been discovered and studied by archaeologists. Two of the most famous, as identified previously, are those from Oseberg and Gokstad, which had been buried for over 1,000 years. The 68 foot (21 meter) Oseberg ship is thought to have been a pleasure craft for sheltered waters because of its shallow draft, but the 79 foot (24 meter) long Gokstad ship may have been a raiding vessel.

Gokstad Ship

The Gokstad ship is made of wide oak planks with a stepped mast. It has a double-ended bow that sweeps gracefully to a high stem or stern. The ship has no carvings but is superbly designed for speed.

Oseberg Ship

Apart from the beauty of its design, the Oseberg ship is superbly carved from stem to stern. The carvings are mostly of animals. One historian wrote:
> No one who has ever looked at the Oseberg ship can ever again think of the ninth century Norsemen as completely vile and soulless barbarians.

Detail of wood carving showing the Saga of Sigurd Favnesbane. After the forging of the sword, Gram, it is tested and breaks.

Right: many of the Viking ships were beautifully carved from stem to stern.

Going Places: Transportation, Exploration, and Communication

The shortage of good farmland in Scandinavia and the desire for wealth and possessions, which could be traded or seized in other lands, prompted the Vikings to venture out from their homelands. They learned to build fine ships to enable them to do this. The map above shows the extent of the Vikings' travels.

Their wide-beamed trading ships, called **knörr**, brought to the north gold, silver, ceramics, glassware, fine fabrics, jewels, and wine. These items had been traded for bearskins and other furs, walrus ivory, reindeer hides and antlers, amber, wax, and slaves. The West Vikings sailed to the British Isles, along the Atlantic coast, and into the Mediterranean. The East Vikings made their way down navigable rivers in small boats, always making sure that they returned before the northern rivers

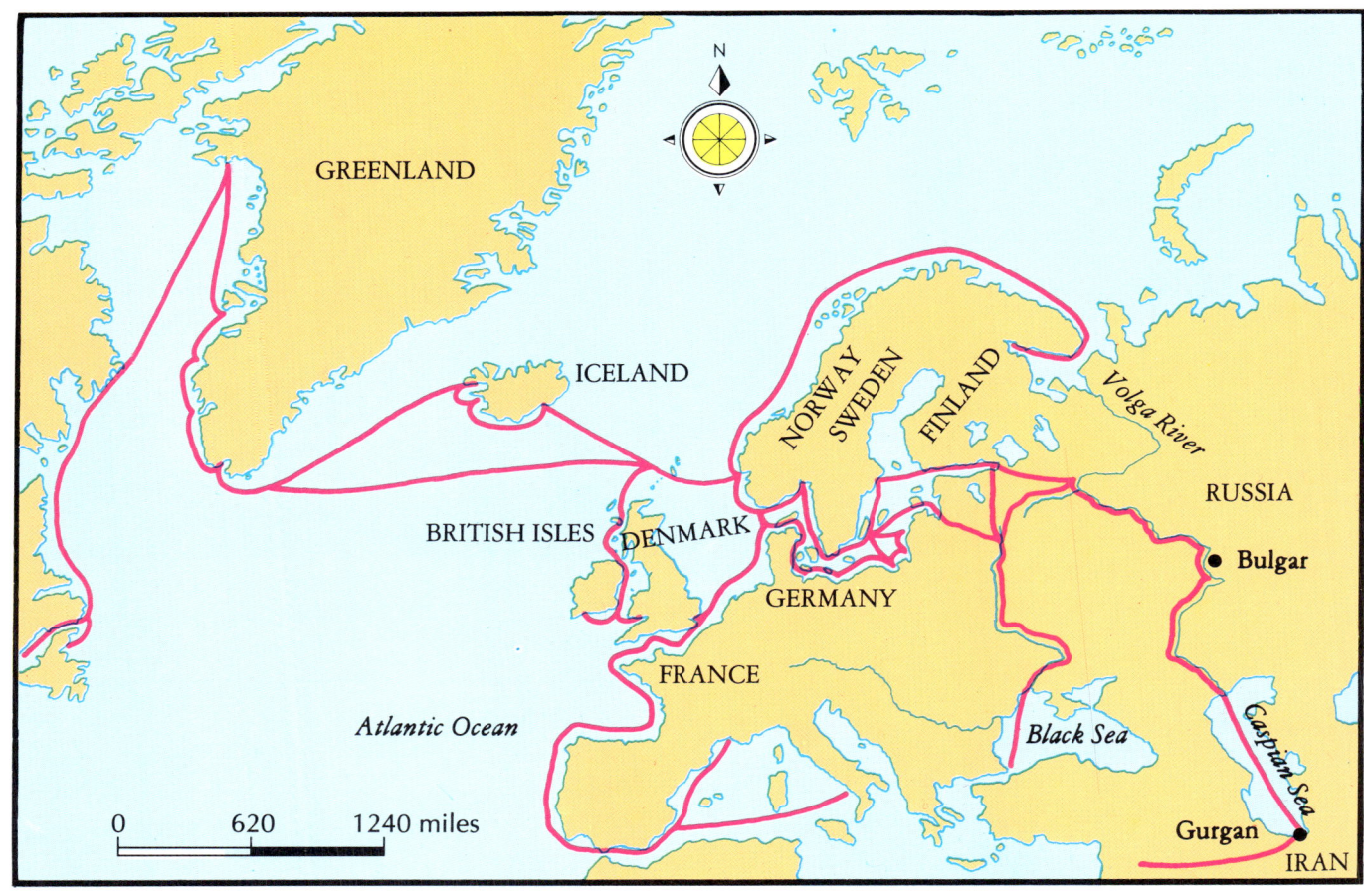

Viking trade routes.

froze in winter. They traveled down the Volga to Bulgar, where they built a temporary trading village of wooden huts, paying one-tenth of their slaves for this privilege. From here, they were able to send out trading parties, who finally reached Gurgan in Iran.

Other items exchanged in Viking trade were horses, honey, malt, wheat, whale oil, butter, spices, arrows, fish teeth and fish lime, hawks, coins, hazelnuts, cattle, swords, and soapstone pots, axe-heads, silks, millstones, and coins. How much of the Vikings' wealth was obtained by way of trade and how much by plunder, piracy, and looting is difficult to know. Trade was peaceful, but we know that the Vikings were not always peaceful.

Detail from carved funerary stone from Gotland, Sweden, shows a Viking ship with a checkered mast.

Viking scales—equipment of a merchant.

Raiding and Plundering

We know from the accounts of monks in monasteries in France, England, and elsewhere, and from the sagas, that the Vikings landed, raided, destroyed, and looted along the coastlines.

Colonization

Although little is known about the earliest Norse settlements, from A.D. 780 on, they appear to have been peaceful and not concerned with plundering and looting. New territories were explored in search of farm and pasture land where a home could be established and a farm life carried on similar to life in Scandinavia. The main colonies were explored, founded and taken over after A.D. 860.

In England the Danes conquered much of the northeast, and took and bought land from the English. Peaceful settlements or colonies were established. Other parts of Europe, such as Normandy in France and Staraja Ladoga in Finland, were settled in the same way.

The urge to explore eventually sent the Vikings out to discover Iceland and Greenland, where settlements were established. Thousands of emigrants left Scandinavian homes, packed their belongings and animals into a boat, and set sail. Entire families were quite prepared to face any danger and settle in new and strange lands. Some of these voyages in open boats lasted seven days or longer.

The Vikings had discovered North America long before Christopher Columbus. The Icelander Bjarni Herjolfsson, in A.D. 986, was the first European to see North America, and Leif Eriksson, on Bjarni's ship, later visited North America on his own.

To enable them to reach their destinations and ensure a safe return, the Vikings were masters of sea lore. They learned the meanings of different cloud formations, the color of water that might indicate shallow areas or rivers flowing into the sea from nearby land, and the closeness of land by the numbers and kind of sea creatures, birds, driftwood, seaweed, and the feel of the wind. The Vikings invented several primitive **navigational** devices, such as the **sun board**, the **shadow board**, and the **sunstone**. They did not have maps or magnetic compasses.

Music, Dancing, and Recreation

Entertaining each other at feasts was a favorite pastime of the Scandinavians, especially during the long winter months. Such feasts were very elaborate with the best food and drink being offered, and people would wear their most beautiful clothes and jewels. Skalds (visiting storytellers) would entertain people with stories, poems, and ballads sometimes accompanied by music. The simplest musical instruments used were rattles, flutes, whistles, harps, long wooden trumpets, and fiddles. We know very little about the songs of the Vikings, for like everything else in Viking culture, these would have been taught by word of mouth. Neither are details of dances known. But the writings of the missionaries tell us that the Vikings did sing and dance, especially at festivals. The missionaries did not approve of the Viking dances and discouraged and forbade them.

Games

In the evenings, especially long winter evenings, families played board games. The Vikings had board games similar to checkers and chess. Outdoor games included ball games and fencing. A games cabinet, designed to be used as a checkerboard, and checkers were found on the Gokstad ship.

Hunting was a recreational activity as well as a way of obtaining food supplies. Hunting and racing hawks were kept, as well as magnificent white hunting falcons.

Skiing

On land the people of the north were expert at traveling over ice and snow, usually to hunt. It is known that the Vikings were using skis in the tenth and eleventh centuries A.D. and Norse myths mention Ull (sometimes Skade), the ski god, and Undurridis, the ski goddess. The oldest skis in the world have been found in the bogs of Sweden and Finland and are believed to be 4,000 to 5,000 years old. Cave paintings dating from 2000 B.C. in Norway also show people on skis.

These late Bronze Age trumpets, called Lurs, were discovered in a peat bog in Denmark. Little is known about the music that was played upon them.

Wars and Battles

Battles, including family feuds, raids, and fights in defense of property, were constantly being waged by the Vikings. There was no permanent army. Every male from fifteen years of age was taught to fight, and each accepted, without question, that he should do so. When a lord (or jarl) wished to raise an army or a raiding party, he would send out war arrows. When a farming community or village was summoned in this way, the eligible men would depart at once with their weapons of axes, spears, swords, arc bows and arrows. Men from a community would form a fighting unit because they could recognize each other by sight. Some fighting units could be as small as sixty men or as large as four hundred. After a battle or raid, those who had fought would receive a share of the plunder or gifts from the lord.

Detail from Gundestrup cauldron. It is thought to be a Celtic work brought to Denmark by the Vikings as plunder.

Swords

These were prized possessions which may have been handed down from father to son. Many stories were told about swords, including tales of magic swords and swords that were gifts from the gods. Some had magic charms or runes engraved on them. A sign of peace was to tie the sword in its scabbard with a strap because it meant that a man could not draw his sword quickly.

Shields

Each man in battle carried a wooden or metal shield. A special white shield would be held up during battle to show that the Vikings were ready to discuss terms of peace. If the offering was rejected, the battle would continue.

Some Well-Known Viking Invasions and Battles

When	Where	What Happened
A.D. 789	Lindisfarne, Northumbria, British Isles	A monastery was raided, sacked, and looted.
A.D. 834	Netherlands and France	Raids on market towns.
A.D. 850-860	Ireland	Norwegians already living in the Hebrides invaded Ireland and settled there. The Danes also invaded Ireland.
A.D. 876	York (England)	Norwegians invaded and settled in Northumbria.
A.D. 878	Wessex (England)	Alfred the Great finally defeated the Danish leader, Guthrum, after many battles. The Danes were allowed to settle, provided Guthrum became a Christian.
A.D. 911	Normandy (France)	After battles and invasions, the Viking chief, Rollo, was allowed to settle. Many Vikings eventually married Christian Frankish women. Rollo became a Christian.
A.D. 1030	Stiklastad (Norway)	King Olaf of Norway killed.
A.D. 1066	Stamford Bridge (England)	King Harald Hardraade of Norway killed by King Harold of England.
A.D. 1066	Hastings (England)	The Normans were descendants of the Vikings. Norman Duke William invaded England, thereby becoming King William I of England.

Many of these battles are recounted in the sagas and histories.

Viking Inventions and Special Skills

Shipbuilding

It was in the seventh century that the Vikings perfected the building and sailing of their ships. The design was unique to the Vikings who combined superb craftsmanship, design, and efficiency. They had a keel that was designed to sail a set course, a sturdy mast, and a single full sail that propelled the ship at great speeds before the wind. The sails were of woven coarse wool and were dyed bright colors. The sides of the ships were high to keep the sailors dry and were often **gilded** and ornamented so as to display the owner's wealth and power. When the sail was not appropriate oars were used to make quick landings and departures. Ships for long distance trade and colonization were of slightly different design.

Byzantine and Islamic coins—part of Viking treasures found in burials. The Vikings fashioned their own coins.

Coins

Vikings introduced their own coins to the areas in which they settled. Coins made trading much easier than the old system of barter (exchanging goods for other goods). The record of coins struck by various rulers also helps historians understand when events happened, and the symbols on coins tell us what was important at the time.

Navigational Instruments

Apart from using the North Star at night, the Vikings invented three devices to help them to navigate their ships. These were the sunboard, sunstone, and shadow box.

Sunboard   This board had a dial in the center on which points of the compass were marked. The Vikings took a bearing from the rising or setting sun. Sources also say that the Vikings took readings at noon, as well.

Sunstone   This was a crystal of **cordierite** (also used in jewelry), which changes color from yellow to dark blue when held at right angles to polarized light from the sun, whether the sun is visible or not. This stone would change color on overcast days and even when the sun was 7° below the horizon.

Shadow Board   This looked like a sundial with a board on which concentric circles (circles having the same center) were drawn, and an adjustable center stick. The height of the center stick would be set so at noon the shadow would fall on a particular circle. By keeping the shadow on the same circle each noon the ship would maintain the same course.

Democratic Justice

The Viking Thing, which was, their **democratic** parliament, law court, and meeting place, was one of the first parliaments in the world. It allowed individuals to have some say in the making of laws. The Thing also served the community as a whole and not just the interests of a few. Every free person was given equal rights before the law. The Vikings were also the first people to use a jury of twelve ordinary people to judge if someone was guilty or not guilty.

Parliament Plains in Iceland where the National Assembly, the Althing, met.

Why the Civilization Declined

By the middle of the eleventh century, the Viking Age was over. The weak states that had been conquered by the Vikings three centuries earlier became more prepared. They had raised powerful armies to resist invaders and to drive out the Vikings. The Vikings also were driven out of England.

The trade route to the east through Russia became less popular as the Mediterranean route was reopened following the First Crusade. Good relations between Sweden and Russia also came to an end.

The Vikings came into contact with Christians, who had made their way to the Scandinavian lands and changed the culture. Some of the Viking kings became Christians because they thought that they might have an advantage when dealing with other Christian leaders in Europe. Many Vikings, especially the Norwegians and Swedes, resisted Christianity with its new beliefs and teachings and repeatedly expelled the missionaries who tried to convert them. Some people, such as the Icelanders, practiced both religions. They did not want to become Christian, but because they were at the mercy of the Christian king, Olaf, who controlled their trade, they agreed. Christianity, by its constant preaching, especially against the slave trade and other aspects of the Viking culture, gradually undermined this culture.

The Vikings, too, had changed. The people who went out to establish colonies elsewhere adapted to their new environment, often intermarrying with the people of those lands and adopting their ways.

The Vikings were not conquered and they did not disappear. They changed as the world changed but the legacy of the Viking Age is still with us.

Descendants of the Vikings still exist today; they changed as the world changed around them.

Glossary

Althing The parliament in Iceland established in A.D. 930. It met beside the Oxara River every year. Its advisers formed a legislature called logretta. Lawspeakers would announce the laws of Iceland from the "Hill of Laws."

Archaeology The study of a culture by carefully digging up, describing, and studying the remains of that culture.

Beriberi A painful disease which causes the body to swell. It is caused by not having enough vitamin B_1 in the diet.

Bur A farm building additional to the main building, used for storing equipment or sheltering animals.

Charcoal A product made by burning wood very slowly. Charcoal contains carbon, which blacksmiths used for working iron.

Colonize Establish a settlement in another country or area.

Cordierite A mineral found in Scandinavia. When held at right angles to rays of polarized light from the sun, it changes color from yellow to dark blue.

Democratic When power or authority is given to the people who use it on their own behalf. This is very different from a government where people are told what to do and are unable to make suggestions or change direction.

Drapas Poems in praise of a king composed by a poet who usually lived in the king's court. They usually praised the king's courage and skill in battle and his generosity toward his people.

Eld-hus Name given to a kitchen or cooking house, which was separate from the main building or house.

Fjord A long, narrow arm of sea bordered by steep cliffs. Many fjords exist along the coast of Norway.

Flax A plant with blue flowers. The fibers from the stems were used to make linen (cloth).

Futhark The name given to the runic alphabet; the name is based on the first letters in the alphabet.

Fylgja Animal spirit that was believed to accompany all Vikings.

Gilded Covered with gold or of a gold color.

Glacial valley A valley that has, or has had, large masses of ice and snow. The ice cuts away the earth as it moves down the valley to the sea. When glaciers melt they leave behind sharp, steep valleys.

Heathen A person who is not a Christian.

Jarl A wealthy chief or landowner; earl.

Kapa A long, heavy cloak with a fur hood.

Karl A free person, including all Scandinavians who were not thralls (slaves).

Knörr A wide-beamed Viking trading ship.

Kyrtil A knee-length tunic worn by men. Kyrtils worn for special occasions were often dyed scarlet and trimmed with fur.

Möttul A fur-lined mantle or cloak worn by the wealthy.

Navigational Aiding in navigating or setting and plotting the course of ships.

Runes Letters used to make up the runic alphabet used by the Scandinavians.

Runic alphabet An alphabet used by the Vikings, usually for carving inscriptions on wood or stone. It originally had twenty-four letters but later had sixteen.

Saga A Scandinavian story told by storytellers (skalds) to entertain. Sagas usually told of achievements and events in history or of a family or person. They were part truth and part myth, or completely myth.

Scurvy A disease which makes the gums bleed and swell and spots appear on the skin. It is caused by lack of vitamin C in the diet.

Shadow board A Viking instrument to assist in navigating ships.

Skald A Viking poet or storyteller who traveled from place to place entertaining people. A skald composed poems and stories as well as told well-known tales.

Skalhatts Round, stiff wool hats worn by men.

Skali Name given to a kitchen or cook house, which was separate from the main house or building.

Skyr A dairy food made from creamy curds.

Stofa The main building in a Viking settlement. This building was used for eating and sleeping.

Sun board A Viking instrument used to assist in navigating ships.

Sunstone A Viking instrument used to assist in navigating ships.

Thing A type of Viking parliament and law court which served the immediate area and was composed of chiefs or jarls in that area.

Thrall A slave. Vikings were slave traders.

The Vikings: Some Famous People and Places

ERIK THE RED

Erik Thorvaldson, who in his youth was nicknamed "Erik the Red," was founder of the first European settlement in Greenland and was father of Leif Eriksson. Erik the Red was exiled from Iceland in about A.D. 980 and set out to explore the land to the west, Greenland. He sailed to Greenland with his family and livestock, spent his exile there exploring, and returned to Iceland in A.D. 986.

A return expedition of twenty-five ships was organized, but only fourteen ships and three hundred fifty colonists are believed to have landed in Greenland safely. About 1,000 Scandinavians lived in the colony by A.D. 1000, but many died of an epidemic in A.D. 1002. The rest of the population gradually died out.

LEIF ERIKSSON

Leif Eriksson was a Norse explorer who is thought to have been the first European to reach America. He was a member of Bjarni Herjolfsson's earlier Viking voyage to America. He later purchased Herjolfsson's ship and obtained as much information as possible from him. Then Eriksson set out in A.D. 1001 with a crew of thirty-five. He reached landfall (thought to have been Baffin Island) and named it Helluland. He made his second landfall near Cape Porcupine. The third landfall was at Newfoundland.

He was the second son of Erik the Red and nicknamed "Leif the Lucky." Leif was converted to Christianity by Olaf I Tryggvason and sent by him to convert the people of Greenland.

BJARNI HERJOLFSSON

Bjarni Herjolfsson was an Icelander who first sighted Vinland and who made Leif Eriksson aware of its existence. It is thought that he sighted America while being blown off course on his way to Greenland, which he finally reached. Bjarni Herjolfsson did not go ashore on the new land he had sighted. This was later to be Leif Eriksson's privilege.

KING OLAF I TRYGGVASON

King Olaf was a Viking king of Norway who forced his people to accept Christianity. Olaf was supposed to have fled with his mother, Astrid, to the court of St. Vladimir of Russia when his father Tryggvi Olafsson was killed by Harald Graycloak.

In A.D. 991 he was a party in the Viking attacks on England and in A.D. 995 he became King of Norway. He had been confirmed in his Christianity in A.D. 994. He succeeded in imposing Christianity on his people in some areas. He was killed in the Battle of Svolder about A.D. 1000.

REYKJAVIK

This is the largest town and capital of Iceland. It was founded in A.D. 874 by Ingólfur Arnarson. Its name means "Bay of Smokes" because of the effects of nearby geysers, steaming springs, and boiling mud holes.

FLOKI VILGERDARSON

Floki was a Norwegian explorer and *Vikingr Mikill*, "Viking of note." He set out to find the newly discovered island called Gardarsholm. He sailed from southwest Norway, landing first at the Shetlands, then at the Faroes, and finally in Iceland, which he named. It was to Iceland that the Vikings sailed, not as conquerors, but as settlers.

SNORRI STURLUSON

Snorri Sturluson was an Icelandic poet, historian, and chieftain. He was the author of the *Prose Edda* and also was thought to have been the author of *Egils Saga*. He married an heiress and lived at Reykjaholt (Reykholt) where he wrote most of his works. From A.D. 1220 to 1232 he was the "law speaker" of the Icelandic high court.

He explains the skalds and their poetry in the *Prose Edda*. He retold the old Norse myths. He also wrote the life story of King Olaf of Norway and included this in *Heimskringla*, his history of Norwegian kings from the time of their legendary descent from Odin.

HARALD I FAIRHAIR

Harald Fairhair was a Scandinavian warrior-chief and the first king to claim sovereignty of all of Norway. He succeeded his father, Halvdan the Black, at the age of ten. Ultimately, he was able to unite all the kingdoms of Norway. Many of his subjects emigrated to England when forced to endure Harald's system of taxation.

An account of his life is found in Snorri Sturluson's *Heimskringla*.

HARALD HARDRAADE

He was king of Norway from A.D. 1045 to 1066. He died in the Battle of Stamford Bridge, Yorkshire, England, against the forces of the English king, Harold II.

Harald Hardraade fought at the age of fifteen against the Danes with King Olaf, his half-brother, at the Battle of Stiklastad in A.D. 1030 in which Olaf was killed. He then fled to Russia but returned in A.D. 1045 to rule Norway with his nephew, Magnus I Olafsson. Magnus died in battle against Denmark. Harald expanded the Viking lands to include the Orkney, Shetland, and Hebrides islands. He also established the city of Oslo. In A.D. 1066 he attempted to conquer England but in spite of early successes in battles, his troops were defeated and he was killed.

ISLEIFR

Isleifr, who lived from about A.D. 1005 to 1080, was one of the first Icelandic scholars, who gained his education after the introduction of the Latin alphabet to Iceland. He was first educated and ordained as a priest and later consecrated as a bishop. His school at Skalholt in Iceland remained a main center of learning for many centuries.

ARI THORGILSSON

Ari Thorgilsson, who lived from about A.D. 1067 to 1148, is regarded as Iceland's "father of history." He is credited with having written the history, *Islendingabók, The Book of the Icelanders* and the *Landnamabok, The Book of Settlements*. There are a few other historical works from this period but their authors are not known. Ari was not the first historian. The earliest remembered historian was Saemundr the Wise, who lived from A.D. 1056 to 1133.

Index

A-viking 16
Aegir 23
afterlife 25
ale 19
Alfred the Great 38
alphabet 28-29
Althing 26, 27, 42
America, North 30, 35
animals 12, 15, 25, 32
archaeology 33, 42
architecture 32-33
army 37
art 32-33
Asar 23
Asgarth 23, 25

Balder 23
barley 14
battle dress 22
battle 23, 32, 37-38
beans 15
bears 13, 15
Bifrost 25
birds 13, 15
Black Sea 29
board games 18
boars 15
boats 13, 15
Britain 9, 12, 38
burial mounds 26
burs 16, 42
butter 17, 19
buttermilk 19

cabbage 15
cats 15
cattle 15
celebrations 25
cheese 17, 19

children 17
Christian missionaries 10, 26, 36, 41
Christianity 10, 26-27, 41
Christians 23, 25, 26, 28, 35, 41
climate 9, 11, 12, 19
clothing 15, 21, 22
cod 13
coins 40
colonies 15, 42
colonization 35, 39
communication 34-35
corn 14
cows 17
crops 14, 23, 25
Crusades 41
customs 14

dairy foods 17, 19
Danelaw 27
Danes 9, 35, 38
death 25
decline of civilization 10, 41
deer 13, 15
democracy 40, 42
Denmark 9, 11, 26, 29
disease 19
dogs 15
domesticated animals 15
drapas 30, 42

El-Majurs 9
eld-hus 19, 42
elk 13, 15
emigrants 35
England 9, 10, 23, 26-27, 35, 38, 41
Etruscan 29

Europe 12, 35, 41
exploration 34-35

falcons 15, 36
families 14, 15, 16, 27
farmers 12, 15
farming 12, 17, 35
farms 9, 14, 16
feasts 23, 26
Fenrir 25
festivals 25
Finland 9, 36
Finn-gail 9
fish 13, 15, 17, 19
fishing 15
fjords 12, 42
flax 15, 42
food 17, 19, 36
France 9, 35, 38
Frey 23
Freyja 23
furniture 13, 16, 32
Futhark 29, 42
Fylgja 23

Germany 9, 26
goats 17
gods 23, 25, 30
Gokstad ship 21, 32-33, 36
Gotland 32
graves 25
Greeks 29
Greenland 9, 29, 35
grouse 13

Haakon the Good 26
Harold Blue-tooth 26
headdress 21
Hel 23

herds 14, 15
herring 13
Histories 30, 38
horses 15, 25
houses 13, 16
Hugin 23
hunting 14, 15, 36

Iceland 9, 27, 29, 35, 41
Icelanders 26
invasions 38
inventions 39
Ireland 15, 38

jarls 27, 37, 42
jewelry 21, 40
Jolablot 23
jury 40

Kapas 21, 42
karls 27, 42
King William I 38
kings 25-27, 30, 38, 41
Knorr 34, 42
kyrtil 21, 42

landforms 11
Latin 28-30
law 26, 27, 40
legends 29, 30
lemmings 13
literature 30
Lok 23
long houses 6
lynx 13

mead 19
medicine 19
men 16, 21, 37
Midgarth 23
Midgarthsorm 25
Midsvetrarblot 23
milk 19
Mimir 23
missionaries 10, 26, 36, 41
Mottul 21, 42
music 36

navigation 40, 42
Netherlands 21, 38
Niord 23
Normans 38
Norsemen 9
Norway 9, 11, 12, 29, 30, 36, 38
Norwegians 9, 26, 38, 41

oats 14
Odin 23, 25, 29
Osberg ship 21, 32, 33

parliament 26-27
partridges 13
peas 15
peasants 14
picture stones 32
pine 13
plants 13
poems 28, 30, 36
poets 9, 30
polar bears 15
poultry

rabbits 15
Ragnarok 25
raiding 35, 37, 38
Ran 23
red deer 13
reindeer 13, 15
religion 10, 23-26, 27-28, 35, 41
rituals 14, 23-26
Rollo 38
runes 29, 37, 42
runic alphabet 28-29
Russia 9, 21, 41

sacrifices 23, 25
sagas 28, 30, 35, 38, 42
sailors 22
Scandinavia 9, 34-35
seals 15
seasons 14
shadow board 40, 42
shields 37
shipbuilding 39

ships 9, 10, 18, 21, 25, 32-33, 34, 39
Sigrblot 25
silk 21
skalds 30, 36, 42
skalhatts 21, 42
skali 19, 42
skills 39
skyr 19, 42
slave trade 10, 18, 41
slaves 16, 18, 27, 34, 42
stofa 16, 42
storytellers 9, 18, 30, 36, 42
sun board 39, 43
sunstone 39, 43
Surt 25
Sweden 9, 11, 14, 26, 29, 36, 41
swords 37

temples 25
tents 15, 18
Thing 27, 40, 42
Thor 25, 30
thralls 16, 18, 27, 42
trade routes 9-10
trade 10, 21, 32, 34-35, 40
trading ships 34
transportation 34-35
trout 13

Uppsala 25
utensils 13

Valhalla 25, 32
Vanir 23
Varangians 9
vegetables 15
Vetrarblot 23
villages 16, 27, 37

war 25, 37
warriors 25, 32, 37
weapons 32, 37
whales 15
wheat 14
wine 19
women 17, 21, 27
wood carving 32
writing 28-29

47

Devon Preparatory
School
Library